The Smelly Dog

The Jigsaw Puzzlers

'It really does fit, I promise'

The Smelly Dog

SOCIAL STEREOTYPES FROM THE
Telegraph magazine

Victoria Mather
and
Sue Macartney-Snape

JOHN MURRAY

Text © 2002, 2003, 2004, 2005 and 2006 Daily Telegraph plc
and Victoria Mather

Illustrations © 2002, 2003, 2004, 2005 and 2006 Daily Telegraph plc
and Sue Macartney-Snape

Foreword © 2006 Julian Fellowes

First published in Great Britain in 2006 by John Murray (Publishers)
A division of Hodder Headline

A CIP catalogue record for this title is available from the British Library

ISBN-13 978-0-7195-6883-1
ISBN-10 0-7195-6883-8

Typeset in Monotype Bembo 11.5/15pt by
Palimpsest Book Production Limited, Grangemouth, Stirlingshire

Printed and bound by L.E.G.O. SpA, Vicenza, Italy

Hodder Headline policy is to use papers that are natural, renewable and recyclable
products and made from wood grown in sustainable forests. The logging and
manufacturing processes are expected to conform to the environmental
regulations of the country of origin.

John Murray (Publishers)
338 Euston Road
London NW1 3BH

Foreword

WHEN I FIRST met Victoria Mather, we and the rest of humanity were living in a different world. She was a deb, I was up at Cambridge and, oddly from today's perspective, I belonged enthusiastically to that team made forever ridiculous by their label: The Debs' Delights. It was 1970 and we ran around together in a London that might have been a different planet to the one we know now. There was hardly any traffic, there were hardly any restaurants and the food in all the clubs tasted as if it had been boiling since the war. Then again, burglary was rare and mugging quite unknown. Policemen were polite, regarding the prosperous as their natural allies and not a bottomless source of revenue. Grocers delivered, dry cleaners collected and bank statements came neatly printed in italicised black or, in my case, red. The girls themselves expected a few years of fun, shopping and skiing, cooking directors' lunches or arranging flowers in the more respectable hotels, before settling down with that very special banking baronet and raising dynasties of boys and girls who would be taught, respectively, to shoot and curtsey. Of course it wasn't all cake. It's true that we didn't lock our doors in the country but we also made do with one loo per twenty bedrooms. Pretty kitchens and, worse, comfortable bathrooms were thought common and central heating was still regarded by some, though not by me, as American and rather suspicious.

But there can be no doubt about one thing: it was definitely the Age of the Eccentric. The older generation divided roughly into two groups. There were those who, after coming through the fighting of twenty years before, had decided, with some justification, that life was the only thing that mattered and all convention was so much dribble. They said what they liked, they wore what they liked, they danced emphatically to the rhythm of their own drum. Alongside these free spirits, there was the other group, those who felt that only by observing every custom and tradition of a century before, could the tide of change and disintegration be stayed. I remember walking off a dance floor in Hampshire to be greeted by a tall colonel with a wide, white moustache. 'Do your tie up at once, sir!' he thundered. 'Good God, man! There are ladies present!' When one remembers that 'Can't Get No Satisfaction' had already been released and Jane Birkin was singing 'Je t'aime', it is easy to see that there was a certain schizophrenic quality to the so-called Swinging Sixties, looking simultaneously backwards and forwards as they were, that provided a rich training ground for the student of human foible.

It is no wonder that Victoria, cavorting at the centre of all this, should have become such a student. She would go on to be a brilliant recorder of British human nature. She has certainly always been equal to what life might throw at her. Sometimes literally. I remember my own father accidentally tipping a plate of duck à l'orange down the front of her dress before a ball at the Café Royal.

We have rattled through the years since then, I as an actor, producer and latterly an author and director, she with a rather more coherent career in writing and magazine journalism, and when we met we would laugh at the changes we had been obliged to witness. At some point Divine Providence introduced her to the equally gifted and percipient Sue Macartney-Snape and, once that had taken place, history was waiting to happen. Heaven knows I have enjoyed the books as much as anyone living, sometimes recognising (or thinking I recognise) the originals of their character sketches, and sometimes feeling they are nudging uncomfortably close to home. Finally, I suppose the salient fact about Victoria's and Sue's work is simply this: Social Stereotypes are very, very funny. Because they are hideously, unarguably true.

Julian Fellowes
March 2006

For darling Dad, Ned Sherrin,
a mentor who's always restrained from commenting
on Bubble's and Petal's eau de Peke
V.M.

For darling Mum,
most of whose many and beloved dogs reached old age,
some becoming quite smelly
S.M.-S.

AFTER NEARLY 700 stereotypes and eight anthologies, it is more than 13 years since Social Stereotypes became integral to the *Telegraph Magazine*, whose readers, dog lovers all, consistently write saying that Stereotypes is the first thing to which they turn on a Saturday morning. The Smelly Dog, The Rescue Dog and The New Puppy were favourites amongst those to whom wet-dog is the odour of sanctity.

At the magazine we thank editor Michele Lavery, for her continued confidence in us; Vicki Reid; Denis Piggott; Jeremy Farr and Ajesh Patalay.

At our publishers, John Murray, Caroline Westmore is a comfort blanket, and we are grateful to Roland Philipps, possessor of a delightfully fragrant dog, for commissioning another book in the series; also to Karin Scherer at Hatchards for her terrific support. My mother used to leave me in the children's department at Hatchards with our Labrador whilst she had her hair done.

Many thanks for inspiration for characters within *The Smelly Dog* are due to Carole Bamford; Ann Collett; Daisy Finer; Douglas Gordon; Geordie Greig; Clementine Hambro; Santa and Simon Sebag-Montefiore and Caroline Wrey. My favourite photographer, Simon Upton, and I spotted The Hotel Pianist in the Adlon in Berlin. In the church-related scenes, the creepy cleric (surely a cat lover) bears no relation to the Rev. Peter Dyson, priest in charge of St Mary's Herriard, where I was married. If there were more intellectual, compassionate, fun, irreverent vicars like him, churches would be full.

Victoria Mather
Hampshire, 2006

Horace's affectionate wet-dog shake has topnotes of fox poo

The Smelly Dog

HORACE IS HEAVEN, if not heaven-scent. Yellow of tooth, scrubby of tail and with breath like napalm. His affectionate nature moves in ways mysterious to those for whom his wet-dog shake all over the best sofa is an invitation to a dry-cleaning bill. Valerie Pottinger has come to play bridge, and isn't really a dog person (she has budgies) so Horace's charming, twinkly stare is being met with nervous regard. Is he going to be one of those dogs who does terrible hugging things to her legs, which are clad in a new pair of Sheer Satin ultratights? Really, if Charmian Fitzroy wasn't such a love, and lady of the manor, one couldn't put up with it. Eau de Horace normally has topnotes of fox poo, in which he has joyously rolled, but Charmian says what do you expect, now that hunting has been banned?

Charmian collected Horace from the Dogs' Home, Battersea, when he was even leggier and scrubbier. It was the eyes. Also his dear tail could double as a gun cleaner. He drooled grateful love over the gearstick all the way down to Kent, then leapt out of the car and made straight for the compost heap, emerging with earrings of fetid grass clippings. Charmian was delighted she had rescued a dog with a sense of humour. Horace and the gardener have a benign war of attrition: the gardener boxed in the compost and Horace has retaliated by swimming frequently in the goldfish pond. The weed has a particularly rich aroma when dried on to Horace's coat. Bits of green frond emerge when he wriggles on Charmian's bedcover at night, all four feet in the air, working his way up towards the pillow via a good back-rub. Mrs Pottinger would faint. But Horace is a beacon of loyalty, a fragrant personality. Anyone who said Horry was horrid would be given watered gin.

The Fashion Faux Pas

IT IS THEIR worst nightmare. Cerise and Violet are petrified in the paparazzi flashlights. The glamour of the Baftas, the red carpet, breathing the same air as Heath Ledger — it's all now dust and ashes in their downturned mouths.

Tomorrow they are going to be a diary item, and not in a good way. Violet, who's had her blonde-mouse hair triple-blonded and wafted into what she thinks is an Audrey Hepburn chignon, is wondering how her stylist could do this to her. To HER! The partner of the director nominated for the best short film in Welsh. Cerise, girlfriend of the assistant to the assistant to the cinematographer working in black and white, blagged the frock from Shelley, her best mate who's on work experience at Karl Popinjay Couture.

Now, both Cerise and Violet want to die. They think as one that it might be different if they were wearing the same dress as Keira Knightley, but to be in the same dress as *this* person, whoever *she* may be, is so not on. Cerise thinks Violet is a horse-faced, stuck-up bitch, with her long nose and her yellow diamond earrings. Borrowed, of course. Violet thinks Cerise may be, horrors, from a soap opera.

Conversation is naturally impossible. They can hardly say 'Nice dress,' can they? And the necessity of getting as far away from each other as possible is rendered hopeless by the press of the crowd. Already they've had to endure one of the Special Visual Effects nominees saying, 'Hey, girls, I didn't know a remake of *Twins* was up for an award,' and falling about at his own joke, burping champagne breath.

In the blinding humiliation of the moment, what neither Cerise nor Violet has realised is that she should never, ever have left home wearing a black lace doily in the first place.

They should both never have left home wearing a black lace doily

In the age of the tieless he is a vision of silk-knotted probity

The Fine Art Auctioneer

IVAN IS SMOOTH as cream. He is, after all, in the business of parting people from very large sums of their money, but in a gentlemanly way. The unpleasantness of vulgar commerce is dressed up in Savile Row tailoring (actually made for Ivan by Sam in the Mandarin Oriental Hong Kong, where he goes to butter up his Chinese clients). In the age of the tieless he is a vision of silk-knotted probity. Only his hair is a little raffish, perhaps to inspire American billionaires' wives with fantasies of running their fingers through it and thus reach for their paddles as he flirts with his gavel.

Throughout the auction of marine paintings the telephone bids, like the chirruping of furious small birds, indicate Ivan's success in charming Japanese buyers. Nothing in his suave demeanour on the dinner-party circuit indicates that modern taste has made life rather tiresome in the fine art department of Christoby's. Only the other day he had to take Buffy Littlehampton out to lunch at Wilton's to let him down gently about his family portraits. Very worthy, school of Van Dyck, but no one wants instant ancestors any more. Minimalism requires an acre of white canvas, with perhaps a strategically placed smattering of orange, as if the artist had been sick. Of course the Impressionists still sell for Japanese boardrooms, but finding an Old Master in the attic of any of the country houses to which he is regularly invited is hardly worth the trouble.

Hence he has ratcheted up the charm a few notches. Ivan values his invitations to Bunbury and Damp Court (he only does houses with single names, or, at a pinch, Court or Park after them), and is a frightfully good shot. Once the season's over, Ivan is off to Moscow. Russian art is the apex of fashionability. He is confident that being called Ivan will be an advantage.

The Blob

NADINE HAS JUST been sacked by her personal trainer. By text. This is the outside of enough, particularly as she was paying the brute £70 an hour. Only a chocolate truffle is going to make her feel better about herself. The diet can begin tomorrow.

All Gary ever did anyway was inflict pain and suffering, making her use the horrid machines she bought at the beginning of January. They were in Peter Jones's window, their spartan hideousness reproaching passers-by for being unfit and unworthy. What are they now doing in Nadine's sitting room? Why did she allow Gary to make her buy a giant yellow ball thingy that looks like a prop from *The Prisoner*? Upon which she had to bounce in her pink Juicy Couture tracksuit. She never liked that either.

Perhaps Gary has sacked her because she looked like a velour boil. 'I feel u lack commitment 2 yr goals,' he has written. Has personal training crossed over into the wetlands of counselling? Nadine may be a little challenged in the waist department, but Gary has dismissed a woman with false eyelashes enhanced with real mink.

Nadine − consoled by another chocolate plus a glass of wine − hasn't been the sort of size 16 to descend into black bin-liner wear. Big jewellery, bright colours, Manolos (possibly not so Gwyneth on swollen ankles) − this is the up, positive way to approach the large side of life. The vast expanse of red can, admittedly, be quite claustrophobic for others trapped with it in a lift.

Well, Gary and his route marches through Battersea Park are in the past. Nadine regrets ever apologising for her wobbling jog and wheezy breathing. Goodbye freezing Battersea, hello Chiva-Som in Thailand. Nadine is going to embrace the spa experience, mind-body-spirit, imbibe wheatgrass, be wrapped in yoga knots. She'll smuggle in a few chocolates just in case it's all too much.

14

Her personal trainer sacked Nadine because she looks like a velour boil

All is not harmonious. The PC squib of a vicar disapproves of 'Onward, Christian Soldiers'

The Village Choir

IT IS THAT time of year again. After ploughing the fields and scattering the good seed on the land for Harvest Festival – Miss Trimble did a lovely descant for the refrain – the village choir is girding its loins for Remembrance Sunday. All is not harmonious. Miss Trimble and Mr Oliphant are adamant that they want 'Onward, Christian Soldiers'. The Rev. Tumbleweed is not convinced; surely it is a little militant? Wringing damp white hands, he suggests 'Abide with Me'. Miss Trimble, beads throbbing on her bosom, says 'Abide with Me' is all very well but what's needed is good rousing stuff. Think *Mrs Miniver*. The rendition of 'Onward, Christian Soldiers' at the end of that splendid film had never failed to reduce her to tears.

The thought of Miss Trimble sobbing quite shakes timid Mr Hopgood, who's been with the choir since 1974, overseeing the recent arrivals of young Jason, and Natasha Ripple, the village schoolteacher, whose creamy soprano has much enhanced church attendance. All are at one with Miss Trimble in thwarting the lefty squib of a Tumbleweed. 'We can't have "Lord of the Dance" every bloody Sunday, Reverend. Remembrance Day isn't feel-good, it's feel grateful we're free English folk, not slaves of the Hun.'

The vicar wonders quite how Mr Oliphant is going to fare on the choral trip to Dresden for Bach's Passion. Tenors are hard to find, so his middle-class commuter-think opinions have to be tolerated – 'After all, we are a broad church' – but Mr Tumbleweed's revenge will be a sermon on political correctness. Christian soldiers will go marching as to war because Mrs Weaver the organist says so, otherwise she's not playing. 'And you can keep your "Abide with Me", we're having "Jerusalem".' The choir's next battle will be preserving the rich man in his castle and the poor man at his gate for 'All Things Bright and Beautiful'.

The Cricket Fan

FROM THE MOMENT Bertie puts on his bacon-and-eggs MCC tie, all seems right with his world. The old arthritis is definitely not giving him so much gyp this morning. It is a fair approximation of a spring lamb that skips off to the match with all the kit required to counteract the vagaries of the English summer: battered Panama, brolly, rug and picnic including a Thermos of hot soup. Plus field glasses, the newspaper so that he can do the crossword during any lull in play, and a transistor radio with earphones for listening to Blowers's commentary.

He is a happy man, having read in the deaths column that a chap shuffled off the mortal coil listening to the cricket scores. What a marvellous way to go. As he tells his dear Dorothy (off to play golf today), cricket's not a game, it's a metaphor for life. It's about fair play and stiff upper lips, it is about respect and teamwork, graciousness in victory and stoicism in defeat. A sniff of linseed oil and Bertie is transported back to the days when he anointed his bat at the beginning of the season and strode out in spotless white flannels to thwack leather with willow for the First XI. He will never actually forgive the one-eyed idiot who gave him out lbw against Charterhouse in 1948, from a ball pitched 18 inches outside the leg stump, but his lip was rigid when he left the pitch.

Today Bertie will chew the fat about the terminal decline of the Test match, that leisurely unfolding of great drama – days away from Dorothy – now steamrollered by the new Twenty 20 matches. And what's happened to England and Flintoff since the Ashes? You never saw pictures of Len Hutton kissing a baby. These are weighty matters Bertie will discuss over a Pimm's. And there goes a six. 'Good shot, sir!'

Cricket's not a game, it's a metaphor for life

*Dede thinks eBay's like a car boot sale without the bother
of going to a muddy field*

The eBay Addict

'CONGRATULATIONS – YOU'RE THE winning buyer' are the words for which Dede obsessively checks her laptop. The six-day bidding war for a black Hermès Birkin bag with silver fittings, in its original box, was so intense that she kept popping down to click on her e-mail in the middle of the night. The euphoria of 'eBay bid confirmed', the nail-biting excitement as the hours ticked down, and ultimate thrill of purchase were somewhat dissipated by the serpentine financial machinations required to pay for it. 'Dear DedeB1980, you have committed to buy this eBay item from ejo264' is all very well, but Dede challenges Gordon Brown to make PayPal work. She eventually summoned her husband's computer nerd, at £100 an hour, fibbing that her Apple Mac had crashed, and got him to sort it out. An efficient woman, Dede never thought she would implore a boy wearing a T-shirt reading THE GEEK SHALL INHERIT THE EARTH not to tell her husband about her secret eBay life.

It's like partaking in a sanitised car boot sale without the bother of going to a muddy field. Dede tells herself it's a global marketplace based on trust, which makes her feel modern and philanthropic. She has photographed and sold all her dud clothes. Much more convenient than taking them to Second Hand Rose and getting a parking ticket.

All this takes an astonishing amount of time, particularly the trips to the Post Office queuing behind suspiciously able-bodied people claiming benefits. So far she's sent off parcels of her cast-offs to California, Iceland and Tanzania. Although why anyone would want a hot and hairy fake Chanel jacket in Africa is puzzling. If Dede can sell her vintage Catherine Walker balldress she'll have a splurge in watches – there are three days to go on an adorable Cartier – and she must somehow fit in Sainsbury's and the school run.

The Pony Club Camp

THE DISTRICT COMMISSIONER tells the mothers they must absolutely on no account leave mobile phones with their children, 'No buts, Mrs Pettifer, little Holly will stop crying as soon as you leave. It is a pity that her pony has just bitten her on the shoulder, but no blood has been drawn. We'll take that bruise in the shape of Moonbeam's teethmarks as a badge of courage, won't we Holly? Now off you go, Mrs Pettifer, and don't forget you're on carrot-peeling duty in the mess tent tomorrow.' North Chalfont Pony Club prides itself on three hot meals a day, ever since Caroline Lindsay took over the kitchen committee after Mrs Cameron's Scottish frugality resulted in a week of fishpaste baps. Mrs Lindsay actually brings chocolate brownies for tea. 'No trouble, we're only 12 at home at the mo, so the cook has nothing much to do.' Georgie Lindsay gets off lightly when a smuggled mobile trills in the pocket of her hacking jacket during dressage. Georgie has a horse lorry with a TV, so everyone wants to be her friend – they creep along from their tents clutching duvets and Snickers bars so they can watch DVDs until midnight.

Everyone thinks Amanda Pilcher is a stuck-up slimebag – she has a groom at home, so can't do anything for herself and lets her team down in the tack-and-turnout competition. Georgie Lindsay and Johnny Somerley squeeze chocolate fudge sauce all over Pilch the Pill's pyjamas. At the end of the week, Moonbeam has kicked the district commissioner, but redeemed himself by carrying Mrs Pettifer to victory in the flag race in the mothers v. children tournament. The battery on the Lindsay lorry is flat because Georgie has watched too much television, and all the children are completely filthy, with pony nuts in their hair. On the last night Georgie, Johnny and Holly stuff bananas up all the instructors' exhaust pipes.

'No mobile for little Holly, and no buts, Mrs Pettifer.
Off you go'

When Gardenia's husband died, she telephoned the estate agent
before the undertaker

The Bulldozer

GARDENIA IS BEARING down on her friend Joyce with bossy intent. 'Now, dear, you've been widowed a year, high time to get over it, take up new pursuits – golf, bridge, art tours to Florence – and you really must move house.' Joyce doesn't want to move from her marital home, full of happy memories and joint endeavour, but Gardenia's overpowering presence in the hall is making the walls close in. The blue floral suit throbs, as if advice was being barked at Joyce by a sofa. 'The garden is far too big for you to cope with, and your daily is quite hopeless.' A scarlet fingernail draws a line in the dust. 'One can't get the staff in the country, you'd be much better off nearer Cheltenham. I have a marvellous Croatian.'

Dear Gardenia, she means well and is so frighteningly efficient. When her husband died of sheer exhaustion, she telephoned the estate agent before the undertaker. Now she's in a modern Georgian crescent with proper insulation because it's silly to waste money on fuel bills. On Mondays she has her hair done, Tuesdays is meals on wheels, every third Wednesday is book club, Thursdays is bridge, Fridays is Waitrose. When there is a proper exhibition in London, like the Stubbs, she books supersaver train tickets weeks in advance and summons Joyce to accompany her 'because otherwise your brain will rot'. A comfortable amount of money and her awesome organisational powers mean Gardenia has plenty of time to tell other people what to do. It is no coincidence that her son has moved to New York and her daughter to Sydney. For want of her grandchildren to terrorise into good behaviour, Gardenia descends on her friends. Joyce proffers a timid glass of sherry – 'It would be much improved if you kept it in the fridge, dear' – and thinks how much pleasure it is going to give Gardenia that the quiche is burnt.

25

The Bored Host

LORD BUZZARD CAN'T imagine why all these damn people are here. He would never dream of going out to someone else's house on a Saturday night, or indeed any other night if he could possibly help it. Far too old to make new friends. 'Eagle' Buzzard drew a line under his friends, other than gamekeepers, after Eton and Oxford. He vaguely recognises some of the assembled throng in the Green Drawing Room as his neighbours; presumably the other whey-faced fools belong to their house parties. He stoically harrumphed when introduced to them, without any intention of remembering their names, or introducing anybody to anyone else. People should know each other already. Really, it is too bad of Euphemia to have asked this crowd, but Lady Buzzard was adamant. 'The Sackvilles are having a dance, Eagle, for the young, in a marquee.' Of the festering inventions of the devil, the young, dances and tents rate next to the French in Lord Buzzard's lexicon.

He is now standing fallow, one leg bent like a horse in a meadow, thinking about pheasant rearing and his new pens in Spring Wood. He is only aroused from this agreeable reverie by Trundle announcing dinner. And so he stumps down to the Yellow Dining Room with Margot Stout; sensible woman, knows all about Cotswold Legbar hens, about which they have a brisk discussion while passing the Giottos in the Long Gallery. Such a mercy, nothing annoys Lord Buzzard more than some simpering female from London asking him about art. Or worse, a jackanapes in a hired dinner jacket saying, 'I've heard so much about the Castle Buzzard library.' He's instructed Trundle to decant Rioja for these fly-by-nights, reserving the Pomerol for his end of the table. Afterwards, the jackanapes busily tell their acquaintances that Lord Buzzard is a marvellous old card.

Lord Buzzard is thinking about pheasant rearing

Splodge is shaken by her bill for wonky carrots

The Organic Farm Shop

ONCE WHEN SPLODGE went to stay with friends in the Cotswolds, Saturday mornings were devoted to antiquing in Stow-on-the-Wold. The new temple of retail is Daylesford Organic. 'You'll absolutely love it, marvellous wonky carrots, candles scented with vine tomatoes, and as for the Turkish pine honey from the uncultivated forests of the Datça Peninsula – Splodge, you'll die. It quite cured Rupert's cold. Didn't it, Rupert?' Rupert, mouth full of bacon from happy pigs and eggs which had convincing amounts of feathers and poo on them, nods enthusiastically.

Flappy says she'd love to go to Lady Bamford's farm shop. 'Everyone is talking about Daylesford, although we have the Marchioness of Douro's new shop near us at Stratfield Saye.' Squiffy can't wait to go, what fun it will be, 'even if in Derbyshire we've had the Chatsworth farm shop for yonks.' Rupert says that Jessica should definitely take the girls to the farm shop, then join them for shooting lunch. 'Bye, darling, you'll all have a brilliant time with barrel-aged feta cheese.'

When they arrive, squeezing Jessica's Land Cruiser beside serried ranks of BMWs, Mercedes and Bentleys, Splodge is overcome by the number of very thin women buying enormous amounts of food. The exquisite pale-green paintwork, the staff aproned in fabulous linen, the perfect orbs of buffalo mozzarella: it is a gourmet Dolce & Gabbana. The Glos posse, in jeans and shearling coats, are buying more than they weigh in kilos of organic veg (to juice) and arcane British cheese made by Mr Nicelittleman, which they'll throw away on Monday because it's dairy. Splodge is sadly shaken by her bill. 'Darling, no additives, invest in your health. And the grouse was really brilliant here this year. Only £10.'

An effete New York interior decorator is not Lady Watkyn-Bassett's idea of a proper person

The Uninvited Guest

GRAYSON HAS BEEN brought to the Watkyn-Bassetts' party by Charles and Edwina, who are now sneaking out the door, leaving him scoffing all Viola Watkyn-Bassett's canapés. An effete New York interior decorator with a beard is not Lady W-B's idea of a proper person, but Charles and Edwina couldn't think what else to do with him. Charles desperately needs Grayson's support to launch his furniture business in America, and they'd shown him the inlaid desks Charles makes in the barn (one has to do something now the EU has made real farming impossible).

Yet nothing made Grayson's beady little eyes light up until he spied 'Lady Watkyn-Bassett At Home' engraved on stiff card on the chimney piece. Grayson believes that he is a modern Truman Capote, confidant of Rockefellers and Rothschilds, duchesses and principessas. Since he doesn't know any, Lady Watkyn-Bassett will have to do. He is now bemusing her with his account of the Costume Ball at the Metropolitan Museum, to which he didn't go, despite implying that he was with Anna Wintour. The nearest Sir Watkyn Watkyn-Bassett gets to grasping Anna Wintour's importance is as some disastrous form of climate change.

Neither the hosts nor the uninvited guest are gaining common ground. *Le tout* Herefordshire wants to talk about how marvellous hunting has been since the ban, but Grayson is in full flow about buying Eames chairs on eBay. This is lost on people whose chairs were sat in by their grandfathers. A little panic is setting in about how this cologne-scented personage is going to be wafted from their midst. Fortunately, Charles and Edwina were not so heartless as to leave without ordering a taxi for Grayson, a small price for deciding that doing business with him would be worse than amputating their own legs with nail scissors.

'Tell this little man how lucky he is that I am considering his wares'

The Ruthless Bargainer

MRS JOHN D. ROTTWEILER III is not going to be ripped off by some smelly carpet seller. Thus the distinguished classics scholar, who thought he was employed to illuminate Mrs Rottweiler about the rock-hewn churches of Cappadocia, finds himself translating Turkish lire into dollars. 'Far too much,' Mrs Rottweiler barks. 'He must think I'm made of money.' As the Forbes listing for Mr Rottweiler reveals this to be precisely the case, the scholar is left stuttering, '*Hali almak istiyorum* (Carpet to buy want I)' without conviction, but with the certainty that he is going to have to carry the beastly thing if Mrs Rottweiler moves in for the kill.

Her Mediterranean cruise had seemed such an opportunity for an impoverished academic: the castles of Patara, the ancient city of Pergamum, the marble ruins of Ephesus, yet he has become a personal shopper. Ditto expert minds hired in Paris, Florence, Prague, St Petersburg (serpentine negotiations about icons) and Venice. The Tintorettos could go hang; Mrs Rottweiler stoutly waddled on to her personal water taxi and demanded to be taken to Murano, and not any old bit of it either, but to Archimede Seguso. Surely John Julius knew young Antonio Seguso makes glass for Cartier and Tiffany? That Mrs Rottweiler has no need of another set of hand-blown Martini glasses in any of her abodes in Manhattan, Palm Beach or Rhode Island is immaterial. It is the thrill of the chase, the opportunity to say that she acquired any admired object in an exotic place, outwitting sly natives.

The soft dollar has distressed her greatly, undermining her bargaining power to crush recalcitrant shopkeepers into submission. 'I have five Picassos and two sets of Meissen. Tell this little man how lucky he is that I am considering his wares.' Mrs John D. Rottweiler III has never paid retail for anything.

The Rescue Dog

ENGINEER HAD A long, sad stay at the Lucky Dogs' Home. Despite the veterinary nurses pinning heart-rending notices on his cage saying, 'I'm not fierce, I'm just ugly, but beautiful on the inside', those in search of canine companionship passed him by in favour of the fluffy and the waggy.

Engineer, of determined character and indeterminable breed, was not going to wag his stumpy tail to curry favour with anyone. Then Bill came around, with a demeanour as uncompromising as Engineer's, terrifying tattoos and a big soft heart inside his beer belly. Engineer bestirred himself from his foursquare stance on the concrete kennel floor and investigated his doppelganger through the cage. And so they went home together to Bill's council house, and a stern masculine life on Bill's allotment, or in the park on the way to the pub.

Bill's wife Iris is respectful of Engineer, which is as it should be, and the lads stick together. Engineer shares Bill's views on Tony Blair ('tosser'), David Cameron ('smug tosser'), and Victoria Beckham ('so pneumatic, it must be like shagging a lilo'). While Engineer does his bit of digging on the allotment, Bill says his bit about bird flu which amounts to believing it when he sees the ducks in the park taking Lemsip. Both appreciate the changing seasons: Engineer takes his time sniff-sniffing the torrid park bedding.

Bill gives him a manly pat: 'For someone abandoned on the inner ring road, you're a right nature lover, Engineer.' Engineer pants fruity breath, and takes Bill to the pub. Bill's not as young as he was, but no feral youth is going to mess with him while Engineer is at his side. When he's got Bill home, Iris says gently, 'You're a smasher, Engineer', and has cooked him lambs' hearts. Engineer does an embarrassed squirm. He knows he is now indeed a lucky dog.

Engineer is of determined character and indeterminable breed

The Park Avenue Princess

COSIMA IS IRRITATED. Really very cross indeed, although the crossness can only be gauged by her orgy of retail therapy, her face having been frozen into a permanent state of disapproval by Botox. It's too annoying; she allowed her house in the Hamptons to be photographed for *Architectural Digest* and the journalist – English, he seemed so respectable when she met him at the Astors – has revealed that she repainted the den 25 times to get exactly the right shade of eau-de-nil to match the pictures. They'll have to move. Cosima already has an estate agent under starter's orders in Provence, but Cosima's husband, Blaise Amory IV, says he's not gonna live in a place that stinks of garlic, there's no golf course and they don't speak English. Should they be living in London? Should Blaise Junior be going to Oxford? Will the Ralph Lauren show, at which she's sitting in the front row, never start, because she has to get to Tiffany's to buy a present for a baby shower?

Cosima's life is one of small imperatives. At the family cosmetics company, where her plate-glass corner office is filled with orchids, the Cosima Bella line needs a new concept in moisturiser and Cosima Baby requires a gorgeous fragrance for tots. Cosima waggles her Harry Winston diamond engagement ring over jasmine, rose and lavender essential oils and just can't decide. She really has to get home for the dog walker to take Trixiebelle out in Central Park, and to supervise her dinner party. She's themed table settings with party chairs that wear ballgowns: swathes of lavender tulle with shocking-pink bows at the back. All the food is bought in, which reminds her to order organic sandwiches for the private jet. Entertaining is so exhausting. Cosima wishes they were just going to Swifty's for twin hamburgers. 'I long for a simple life,' is what she tells Blaise as her Pilates teacher and her hairdresser arrive.

'I long for a simple life'

The Old-Age Wedding

EVANGELINE LAST GOT married when she was 18, in St Margaret's, Westminster. Her dress was made by Norman Hartnell and she had four fellow debutantes as bridesmaids in floating tulle. When she left her parents' house in Chester Square as a bride, Nanny told her not to fuss, 'because nobody's going to be looking at you, dear'. How different this day is in the Norman church at Chalfont Magna, with Hector gazing at her so adoringly. Dear Julian was a sweetie, but looking at her at all was difficult as he started on the Glensporran malt at 10am. It was cirrhosis in the end.

Evangeline never thought she'd marry again; after all, you just change one person's set of irritating habits for another's. Then she met Hector when they were both taken to *South Pacific* at Grange Opera. He knew all the lyrics – so jolly of him – and had brought an excess of foie gras for the picnic. 'The problem with being a widower is that one's appetite is undiminished and the opportunities for good food fewer,' he confided. His wife, Evangeline discovered from her friends (never from Hector), had fought a valiant battle with Parkinson's. Forged in the mill of life's vicissitudes, Evangeline and Hector became friends, good bridge partners, and both like James Lees-Milne's diaries, Venice in the autumn and pugs.

Now, surrounded by their beaming children, all hugely relieved that their respective parents' loneliness is no longer their problem, Evangeline is attended by eager granddaughters. Hector, a retired colonel, is poignantly upright. The bride's and groom's knees crack like pistol shots as they kneel for the prayers; his hip replacement requires a gentle hand under the arm from his eldest son, the best man. Evangeline reflects that when she first got married she wore one wincy strand of pearls; now she's got a triple row of stonkers, and sapphires, and a Philip Treacy feather.

*Evangeline never thought she'd marry again; after all, you just change
one person's set of irritating habits for another's*

Joanna's blog is personal musings of the Aren't Men Awful genre

The Blogger

JOANNA'S BLOG IS the equivalent of her husband's shed. While Gordon retreats to the end of the garden to do manly things with a Black & Decker workbench, she goes to the spare room – their son's left home – and her laptop. Her blog isn't exactly Boris Johnson noting a vision of Baroness Thatcher in Tory blue wafting through Portcullis House, but personal musings of the Aren't Men Awful genre.

When Joanna started joblog.com with easy-to-use software she hadn't thought there'd be anyone else out there; there may be five million blogs in the blogosphere, but would anyone be interested in the tribulations of an empty-nester married to someone incapable of speech during Test matches, when they could hit the blog worshipping *Buffy the Vampire Slayer*? But Joanna blogged on, confiding Gordon's non-relationship with the dishwasher ('It's next to the sink. Wouldn't it be just as easy to put his mug in the dishwasher as in the sink, who does he think is going to deal with it – the washing-up fairy?') to the world wide web.

Then she met Trudie. Although 'met' may seem strange, as they haven't actually chummed up over a macchiato in Starbucks, but Trudie is now more real to Joanna than her next-door neighbour. She wouldn't dream of telling Mrs Fothergill that Gordon always burped after his supper, patted his stomach and said, 'That was tasty, love', and that it drove her mad. But Trudie is safely in Knutsville, Ohio, and her Rocky picks his feet while he watches TV. Sheila in Sheffield says that's nothing; after Tyrone's had a skinful in The Coal Scuttle he blows his nose on the sheets.

It may not be Salam Pax writing from Baghdad during the Iraq war, but it's frontline stuff from desperate housewives, without the cosmetic surgery. Joanna is actually nicer to Gordon after she's excoriated the poor geezer to her sisterhood in cyberspace. Men!

The Muscular Christian

BISHOP MIKE IS the pop idol of the pulpit. Even those who would be most alarmed to be thought born-again Christians, just being fed up with the vacuity of their local vicars, go to the church of St Jude the Obscure when the Bish is preaching. The man has a brain, thank the Lord, and has been out and about in the world (he was in construction in the Far East).

'I was a late conversion,' he booms, 'which means I've got God and a stainless-steel kitchen.' Pause here for laughter. 'And I have a steely attitude to God. It's simple: I believe. And what I believe in is Real Christianity. Getting down and dirty: forget sherry and bridge at the bishop's palace – you're not living in a Trollope novel – think poverty in Rwanda.'

In no time he has organised pens, pencils and children's books to be sent to schools in central Africa; a demon football player, in his dog collar, he has rustled up a football team to play local teams in Uganda while also seeing mountain gorillas. 'Eco-tourism is a mission, let's help save the planet.' Bishop Mike rejoices in pit latrines, kerosene lamps and cold showers. He knocks back local beer with vigour, sends digital pictures of his flock's journey from passing internet cafes and exchanges high fives with fellow preachers at the open-air church services.

His diocese is harangued to give goats and cattle to the Third World by a Cafod scheme. A slide presentation of dirt-poor urchins playing in open sewers punctuates this appeal – 'They don't ask for an Xbox for their birthdays, they'd ask for clean water. When did any of you actually *need* anything?'

Despite his Far Eastern days having, he says, given him profound respect for the gentle ways of Buddhism, Bishop Mike has a hearty knack of bullying his fellow Christians into guilty submission.

Bishop Mike believes in Real Christianity

*Like a female Nicky Haslam, age cannot wither her
nor the years condemn*

The Age Refusenik

ROSE IS A disgrace. Her contemporaries have long since embraced the pure wool safety of Jaeger, but she is in combats bought in Brixton market. Like a female Nicky Haslam, age cannot wither her nor the years condemn. To some her cleavage might look like crinkled snakeskin, but the young are far too transfixed by her funky jewellery to think her anything other than a cool cat. 'Did you really get that in the souk in Marrakesh, Rose?' 'No, darlings, the night market in Chiang Mai. They sell silver necklaces by weight there; haven't been able to abide Marrakesh since I came across a man selling baby tortoises, all lying on their backs in a cage, little feet flapping. Foreigners can be such beasts.' Political correctitude, along with the words 'mutton', 'dressed' and 'lamb', is meaningless to Rose. She has many dear friends who are maharajahs, all eager to put crumbling bits of their palaces at the disposal of one who so admirably fulfils their idea of English eccentricity, but when in Delhi she usually stays with the mother of the Indian who runs the corner shop at the end of her road. 'Marvellous – she makes tea strong enough for a duck to trot across.' Rose's son, Hugh, is only too pleased his mother isn't rocking up to the Imperial with her backpack.

Hugh hasn't recovered from Rose's arrival at the twins' christening on a bicycle with her skirt tucked into her knickers. That the twins think Rose – always Rose, never Granny – is the magnetic north of fascination is profoundly irritating, particularly to her daughter-in-law, Jane, who says 'One never knows who the twins might meet', as if Rose were a social disease. That Rose's little house is full of artists, student designers, and marvellous, if undusted, antiques cuts no ice with Jane who, coming from Godalming, has a deep suspicion of anyone with non-matching china.

The Villa Party

IT WAS ALL Minkie Montague's idea. She read about this marvellous villa in *Condé Nast Traveller*. So amusing, bedrooms in medieval towers and its own chapel and pizza oven. Over kitchen supper in Wiltshire on a dank February evening, the Montagues, the Chubbs and the von Witters decided to share this gem. They could practically smell the lavender; Kitty von Witter could taste the Soave.

The Montagues played a blinder by flying out the day before, thus arriving at the villa early to bag the best bedroom with the four-poster and balcony overlooking the olive groves. The Chubbs, whose easyJet flight was late, are condemned to the bedroom with the deep freeze in the corner. Henry Chubb is not happy: 'Well, we all know who's getting better value for their £2,000 a week, don't we?' Also he can only receive a signal on his mobile due south of the third cypress tree on the right. There's rippling dissension about who goes to the hypermarket; Minkie says she really feels it is her job to organise their cultural expeditions, and unites herself with the Blue Guide. Kitty says she doesn't mind going a bit, but never seems to make it past Giovanni's Bar Cherubino.

When the swimming pool assumes a delicate Fra Angelico shade of verdigris, Chuffy Montague discovers that the caretaker doesn't care or speak English. Minkie suggests a cheering jaunt to a marvellous Pregnant Madonna and lunch in a little place recommended by Tony Lambton. The von Witters get lost in Montepulciano, the Pregnant Madonna is being restored ('*Chiuso, signora, la capella chiuso*') and the Chubbs resent splitting the bill when Chuffy's eaten steak Florentine while they shared a mozzarella and tomato salad and don't drink at lunchtime. On the way back the von Witters's hire car breaks down. Chuffy's overdone the vino rosso and fails to make the pizza oven work. Back in Wiltshire they all say it was wonderful.

There's rippling dissension about who goes to the hypermarket

The Crossword Addict

GLORIA HAS GOT it. At 3am she woke with a start and knew the answer to 21 down was 'Armageddon'. She also woke her husband with this revelation, who groaned, 'Well done, old girl, now let a chap have a bit of kip.' So she's out of bed, down the Jacobean corridor, dressing gown flying and impervious to the cold, in order to complete the crossword in the newspaper which has been scrupulously folded back – so no one else can actually read the news – and initially filled in with pencil in case the *DNB* lets Gloria down with 19 across.

Not that she would admit to reference books. The solution to the crossword is supposed to come fully formed from her total understanding of the crossword-setter's mind.

Sudoku holds no fascination. Numbers are sterile in comparison to having worked out, in the nanosecond between buttering toast and reaching for the Cooper's Oxford, that the answer to 1 across, 'Tommy plans to use invested income (7,5)', is obviously 'Private means'. The mating call of 'Got it!' is that which echoes across the breakfast table, and Gloria was most annoyed when Eustace announced casually that any fool could see that 7 down, 'Entre nous, the stylus isn't working (3,3,6)', was clearly 'Off the record'. She, however, retaliated with 'Cinderella's midnight music (7)': Ragtime'.

Her grandchildren give her crossword compilations for her birthday, and her son, who's a banker, was thrilled with the complicated electronic crossword gizmo he found for Gloria for Christmas. It's gathering dust. Nothing compares to the exhilaration of the daily newspaper challenge. Gloria gets up at 6am to get to the *Telegraph* before Eustace.

At 3am she realises the answer to 21 down is 'Armageddon'

The Ballboy

BOBBY HAS BEEN through boot-camp training in order to roll a tennis ball in a straight line. Since February he has been attending four two-hour training sessions a week, getting fit, learning the rules of tennis, practising foot movements and correct stance, and acquiring the etiquette of maintaining grace under fire. While other kids festered in front of computer screens, Bobby's been cross-country running, and forged in the maelstrom of modern manners: the towel throwers, the foot stampers, the could-you-not-see-that-was-outers – Bobby can cope, although anxiety ripples up his spine. Comforting Anne Rundle, ballboy matron, has trained the boys and girls for 20 years, with role players acting stroppy behaviour, but who can forget when young Tim Henman lost the plot, whacking a ball that clipped a ballgirl on the ear? At his secondary school in SW19 Bobby was considered dead goody-goody by the hoodie crowd – 'Bet you just want to look at Sharapova's knickers, freak' – but as he's got fit and they've got nowhere, Bobby has got respect. Bobby's on TV. They saw him hand a ball to Federer. Bobby says Federer's really polite and gave him his sweatbands when he won. Wow! How cool is that? That was Bobby standing next to Maria Sharapova – what a babe. But Bobby just says Miss Sharapova is very nice. His parents are bursting with pride: what discretion, what valour, what military precision, what concentration, and his father is relieved that Bobby's duties do not include handing the players cigarettes between sets, as the first ballboys did in the 1920s. Now the weight of the tournament rests on his sloping shoulders. He's the unsung hero, the little sprat bursting across the greensward from baseline to net, a leitmotif of the world's best tennis tournament. Bobby doesn't know about any of that, but he's thrilled to get two weeks off school.

He's the unsung hero, the little sprat bursting across the greensward from baseline to net

Oh joy — they've just threatened a small business with closure under section 1,389 of 'elf and Safety

The Petty Officials

MAVIS AND REG are in transports of joy. They have just menaced a struggling small business with closure because, under section 1,389 of the 'elf and Safety Act (paragraph seven), it is a hygiene hazard to have a kettle in the post room. Mavis distinctly detected limescale. The PA, a blonde, hair-flicking minx, actually said she used fresh ginger to make herbal tea. Reg was in shock. Was the blonde aware of the volatile nature of fresh ingredients? And what, might he ask, was wrong with the teabag?

Anything hermetically sealed in cellophane speaks to Reg. He and Mavis recently reduced the headmistress of a charming kindergarten to tears for reusing open finger paints. Who knew where the toddlers' fingers had been? And what was more, Reg said, nursery staff had been observed by himself and Mavis smoking and drinking Red Bull by the kindergarten's back door. Mavis, the chorus to Reg's death sentences, declaimed that under the council's regulations concerning primary education, carers should be non-smokers. And the evidence of Red Bull (Mavis is a great one for snooping in bins and photographing suspect contents) suggested a rackety lifestyle unbecoming to those in charge of small children.

Having spread fear and despondency among overtired, underpaid young women dedicated to singing 'Do-Re-Mi', Mavis and Reg go off to have a coffee. Reg is appalled by the spoons. Customers enjoying a frothy coffee might have licked them. Is the dishwasher washing to a standard of heat sufficient to kill all known germs?

Reg reflects that few people, other than Mavis, understand the stress of the job. They are on the frontline of public liability. No raised paving stone can be judged to have tripped up an elderly pedestrian without their say-so. Secretly he and Mavis long to be airport security police, forcing people to abandon their tweezers.

The Oversized Bag

NATASHA IS DWARFED by her object of desire. Having been on the waiting list for a Nicole for three years, she is not now going to admit that it is too big, that baby blue is the wrong colour or that, lacking the detective skills of Sherlock Holmes, it is impossible to find one's keys in the bottom.

She has taken the bag to Le Caprice – or did it take her? – and her girlfriends cooed at it and stroked it and, while Natasha was ordering her bang-bang chicken, surreptitiously ran manicured fingernails over the chrome lettering to check it was real.

Crystal van der Vyl said she got the most marvellous fake in Florence, you really couldn't tell the difference, so she bought four in different colours. So much more amusing to have amethyst, and burnt orange, and there was a darling acid green.

Natasha, nursing her bag on her lap in case Nicole thieves are at work beneath the tablecloth, feels quite dull. Her husband complained all Christmas Day about 'having to spend my entire bonus on a bloody handbag'; her son returned from reading environmental awareness at Beard University and asked whether she realised that the price of her stupid handbag could enable an entire African township to have a wind-powered generator. Her daughter said, yeah, well, but no, and, 'Hey, Mum, don't leave that thing on the hall table, will ya. It upsets my veggie friends. Sergei says it must have taken the death of a whole cow to pander to your vanity.'

Natasha has a vivid image of Sergei – Russian father big in fossil fuels – wearing a cashmere poncho. 'But the goat didn't die, see? It was combed.' Natasha wishes cows could be combed for Nicole bags, she really does; she'd also like it not to be quite so heavy when laden with a wallet and a lipstick.

Natasha's husband complained all Christmas Day about having to spend his entire bonus on a bloody handbag

*On New Year's Day all ashtrays were ceremonially
thrown out of the house*

The Quitter

IT IS 11AM. Crispian is now at the pencil-chewing and salt-and-vinegar crisps stage. The worry beads began rattling at breakfast. Pre-breakfast, when he'd normally have had a fag with the *Daily Mail* and a black coffee, he dragged the dog out of its basket and took it for a walk. The dog was livid.

On New Year's Day, as Crispian wheezed down the stairs after Belinda Stukeley's chav party, all ashtrays were ceremonially thrown out. No one is now allowed to smoke; his daughter's teenage friends, used to a cosy fag fug in front of *EastEnders*, are thrust unceremoniously into the garden, where frost is on the bough.

Any intimation of a sneaky Marlboro Light invokes a sanctimonious lecture on the evils of smoking and how he, Crispian, has seen the cross section of a lung, grey and congested by verminous nicotined cobwebs. 'Never again. If you had seen what I have seen, you'd be aware of how you are poisoning your own body. Think of your future. Think of doctors who may refuse to treat you because you are a smoker. Think danger.' Teenagers with low-slung trousers nod tousled blond hair and say 'Whatever' and actually think that Crispian smoked 60 a day and doesn't look such a sick old geezer. Anyway, who'd want to live to be his age? The alcohol will probably get him. Crispian, chewing gum furiously, is frequently to be found delving in the drinks cupboard; a Bloody Mary, very spicy, helps distract the Craving Demon. Possibly two Bloody Marys. That's after the post-breakfast Cokes. A bit of red wine at lunch induces a siesta coma, which whiles away an hour of ciggie-longing.

On Monday he's going to the acupuncturist, followed by the hypnotist. So far he thinks he's doing frightfully well. What about just a cigar in the evening? Of course, he wouldn't inhale.

All are feeling thoroughly ill-used by the little bundle of happiness

The New Puppy

MORIARTY IS GAME on. He's using Tissue, a venerable descendant of the original Andrex puppy, as a trampoline. Tissue is affecting sleep, something of which they've all been deprived since Moriarty's arrival to jazz them up. 'Come on, Mother, a new puppy will revitalise you ancients. Tissue's heading for the basket in the sky, Blister waddles as if he's on a Zimmer frame, he needs a more active life, and Gromit may be Proustian, but is he content? A puppy, a little bundle of happiness, is what you need.'

Letitia allowed herself to be persuaded. Moriarty, bounce-bounce-bounce, was adorable on first acquaintance. Indistinct breed, but the charming personality of all rascals. Also the casual attitude to correct behaviour. Puddles on the Aubusson, puddles on the seagrass carpet (a stain impervious to the curative powers of Perrier water), puddles on the bathmat, which is Moriarty's little joke – how can Letty tell if it's really from her bath? Letty has watched the masterful Victoria on *It's Me or the Dog* but mentioning 'boundaries' and 'routine' to Moriarty has been received with cheerful disinterest. Letty's shoes are shredded, Tissue's blanket has been dragged out on the lawn, Blister's bowl appropriated and Gromit's ears chewed. All are feeling thoroughly ill-used by the upstart, and Moriarty's vomit, comprising phenomenal amounts of sheep poo, was not best positioned by the Aga when the vicar came to tea.

Nor have Letty's hens got off unscathed; Moriarty chases them round the kitchen garden so none of them will lay. The tottering family tortoise, Churchill, emerged from a blameless hibernation to be batted by small paws and have undignified parts of himself sniffed. Mrs Clod, who wheezes up from the village twice a week, says she's not putting up with that puppy's doings in the back passage. In his and her defence Letty says weakly, 'Really, he's awfully sweet.'

The Middle Wife

IMOGEN HAD AN exquisitely successful picture-framing business when she met Alex. Everyone took their pictures to her – Bono, Jacob Rothschild – for Imogen's taste is the epitome of contemporary elegance. She also had a secret weapon: Mikhail, her soulful Serbian picture-hanger, a wizard with the spirit level. Really, no one could hang their modern-art collection without Imogen and Mikhail.

Alex found this desirability by association with the great and the good intriguing. Immy was so restful after his first wife, a raw-boned colonel's daughter who shouted at him, and never failed to make it obvious that she thought him suburban for preferring golf to hunting. Immy was flatteringly receptive to his metrosexual ways: the handmade suits, the moisturiser, the company box at Covent Garden, which she mistook for an interest in opera. He was, she felt, a delicate soul who'd had a dreadful time with That Woman.

Never married before, Immy set out to be the perfect wife, but somewhere in between having the perfect baby (a boy, such a blessing after the bolshy teenage stepdaughters), arranging the perfect flowers and decorating the perfect house, Immy's personality disappeared into the dishwasher. She sold her business, which made his lectures about the cost of the child – 'Entirely your idea, Imogen, Lord knows I never needed another set of school fees' – the nanny, the flowers and the house more unpleasant.

Three years later, Immy is on her own in Montpelier Square, Alex having moved on to Lynn, a hard-boiled American professor of psychiatry who's made him live in a loft space and abandon all his old friends. Alex's daughters now say that Immy was so cool, she took them to Bliss Spa, and Lynn's a stepmonster. 'By the way, Dad, Immy's really happy with Mikhail.'

*Imogen set out to be the perfect wife, but her personality
disappeared into the dishwasher*

*Come the cocktail hour, bosoms heave with jewellery
behind glasses of champagne*

The Hotel Pianist

As TIME HAS gone by Leonard has tinkled 'As Time Goes By' for an eternity behind his palm frond. If any of the ladies who lunch or American tourists who frequent the Grand ask him to play it again, he smiles gallantly at their little joke. Meanwhile, the works of Cole Porter, Irving Berlin, Noël Coward and Andrew Lloyd Webber ripple from his fingers as seamless audio wallpaper. The teatime crowd like a little *My Fair Lady* with their scones and clotted cream. It seems refeened, and tea in the Palm Court is nothing if not refeened. Sometimes he sees small granddaughters wriggling on the gilt chairs, gives them a little wink and plays 'A Spoonful of Sugar' to get them through the ordeal of their treat. Come the cocktail hour, bosoms heave with jewellery behind the glasses of champagne. Leonard may essay a *Blue Danube*, although the assistant hotel manager, Miss Snapper, has warned him not to be too intellectual. Before dinner he sees some of the couples for whom he played at their wedding receptions in the Empress Josephine Room. They wave and mouth 'Hello, Leonard' over the chatter and the undertow of that blasted nightingale singing in Berkeley Square. It's a particular favourite with Lady Montmorency, reminds her of happy days during the war, and she sometimes sends him a drink. Otherwise Leonard continues in anonymity. Some enchanted evening there will come a stranger to take him away from all this, recognise his real talent. He'll be a concert pianist at last – no more Palm Court, hello Carnegie Hall. Leonard's old mother will be able to see him on the telly; there'll be CDs and royal performances. He'll be able to buy a new greenhouse. As yet again he plays 'Memory', dreaming of what might be is a salve. At 10pm, his bow tie in the pocket of his mackintosh, he takes the bus home wondering if all his tomorrows will be measured out by 'Yesterday'.

Blond called out unto blonde

The Matching Couple

WHEN ADRIAN'S AND Annie's eyes met across a crowded wedding marquee it was with the recognition of twin souls. Blond called out unto blonde. Were they in a Richard Curtis movie, the easy-listening soundtrack would have been playing 'All You Need is Love' as they sought each other in the melee of adorable bridesmaids and old aunts with hairy moles.

Actually, they *are* in a Richard Curtis movie. He took her on a weekend mini-break to Babington House. They both love the countryside, particularly if it comes with a spa and a private cinema attached. They both love old movies: on their first date they discovered they could quote *Casablanca* by heart. It was their wedding next, and they bought the house in Notting Hill with the communal garden, and it's all white because they both work in design. Adrian's photographs of India illuminate the study they share: they both love travel. Their honeymoon was at an ashram – they both think health and inner tranquillity is so important. A private meditation guru comes to the house twice a week, and all their vegetables are organic.

Even their dogs, charming blond reflections of their owners, eat free-range meat, nothing from tins. Adrian's and Annie's dinner parties (white plates) are things of fresh asparagus and sea bass, the fishmonger at Chalmers & Gray having been interrogated about whether it has been line-caught. Adrian and Annie do not wish any dolphins to have died in the attempt to provide their meal. They are both eco-conscious and can tell their friends much about sustainable energy sources.

When they speak, it is alternately, finishing each other's sentences. To their friends they have fused into a single entity, Adrian'n'Annie. When they have children, they will be identical twins.

The Churchwarden

MAJOR TODHUNTER (RETIRED) finds Christmas very stressful. Goodwill does not come naturally to one ingrained with military discipline. There has been a touchy-feely suggestion from Sorrel Chipstead, one of those modern mothers, that the children should take up the collection at the Nine Lessons and Carols on Sunday. The Major regards the collection as the churchwarden's prerogative, certainly not to be trusted to the sticky fingers of revolting little brutes. And what will they get up to during 'Away in a Manger'?

The vicar thinks piping childish voices gathered round the crib 'all part of the spirit of Christmas, Major,' but Toddy Todhunter foresees childish candles falling into the straw, a conflagration enveloping the Baby Jesus and, worse, setting light to the newly repaired church roof for which he spent five years raising the funds – funds sweated from the parishioners by bring-and-buys and quiz nights. All a rearguard action against the vicar's unfortunate tendency to favour the Third World.

Charity begins at home, according to the Major, particularly in view of the perilous state of the bell-tower. The bells could well fall through rotting beams at any moment, but now the vicar is saying that we should be giving without thought of self to Pakistan.

But the bells, the bells! Also the heating bills incurred by the midnight service. Otherwise the organist complains of her arthritis – 'You wouldn't want all ye faithful coming and my fingers being too frozen stiff to play, would you, Major?' – and Christmas guests down from London think it amusing to blow breathy clouds in the air. The Major, rectitude reinforced by a thermal vest, will be handing out *Hymns Ancient & Modern*, on which the Archbishop of Canterbury's subversive views stand no chance while Toddy is churchwarden.

The Major regards the collection as his prerogative,
not to be entrusted to sticky-fingered children

'She's such a sweet, co-operative little blossom normally,
Miss Frobisher'

The First Assessment

CHENOWYTH HAS RESOLUTELY refused to tell Miss Frobisher what her name is – admittedly it is a tricky one – responding only by sing-songing, 'I am called Cushion.' Chenowyth's mother is desperate. If Chenowyth doesn't get into Witchbroom prep school, Mummy's credibility at lunches at San Lorenzo will plummet.

Acceptance at the Fairy Glade just implies that Chenowyth is social and thick. She *has* got into Acland's. Everyone gets into Acland's, and the uniforms are dear, with long, swinging red hoods like elves. But Chenowyth's mother is not at all sure about the vegetarian meals at lunchtime, although of course she and Chenowyth's father said how much Chenowyth loved organic cracked wheat. 'She's such a sweet, co-operative little blossom normally, Miss Frobisher. I think it must be the excitement of coming to Witchbroom. She's always playing with Lady Sporran's children, who love it here so much, and we go and stay with Jeremy Tellistar every summer in Capri and his children adored Witchbroom. Come along, Chenowyth, tell Miss Frobisher about when we went to Pompeii! She loves classical civilisations, you know. Next stop Leptis Magna!'

Chenowyth's mother is now in overdrive. While she name-drops to Miss Frobisher, and burbles conversational humdingers including Chenowyth's precocious interest in Plato, Shakespeare and Mozart – 'You must hear her *Eine Kleine Nachtmusik* on the xylophone' – Chenowyth's father is wondering nervously whether being a hedge funder still counts for anything. And Chenowyth certainly isn't doing very well on eye contact. Her mother mentally makes a pact with God to give Miss Frobisher a Chanel handbag next Christmas if only Chenowyth gets into this school that smells of loo brush.

The Hen Enthusiast

KATIE IS AGONISED. The spectre of avian flu haunts the chicken run, already living in fear after the hunting ban. The predations of Mr Fox have required fence-building on a scale normally only deployed in high-security prisons. This has quite ruined the effect of Katie's dear little henhouses, architectural gems designed by an art-student friend who was having a nervous breakdown.

Katie's Frizzles particularly like the oriental pagodas, which are high enough to accommodate their hairdos. The Marins have appropriated the miniature New England clapboard farmstead with its verandah and charming window boxes. Katie plants them with daffodils and the effect at Easter is positively Hallmark-card. Daffs, eggs, fluffy chickens: what if DEFRA decides on wholesale slaughter because some miserable person has sneezed in Asia?

Katie's grip on the DW40 virus leaping from birds to humans is tenuous, but although the chickens do come into the kitchen, particularly when she's boiling up scraps on the Aga to mix with their organic corn, and her favourite Buff Orpington once laid six eggs on the nursery sofa, they don't exactly cohabit. Katie remembers the stinking firepits of the foot-and-mouth epidemic and imagines her chickens roasting, claws up. It is a spine-stiffening thought. Would the Dowager Duchess of Devonshire, who put chicks in glass tanks on the Chatsworth dining table when she published *Counting My Chickens*, give in to bird flu? Certainly not.

Katie has ordered a vast organic turkey for Christmas as a gesture of solidarity with her local butcher. And she doesn't even like turkey. It would never do to eat the hens, much too personal. Upset in the chicken run results in a tragic lack of eggs. Henrietta was sitting on one miserable offering so Katie had to buy free-range eggs to slip into her nest. Henny hatched them beautifully. Clever girl.

Katie's grip on the DW40 virus leaping from birds to humans is tenuous; although her Buff Orpington laid eggs on the nursery sofa, they don't cohabit

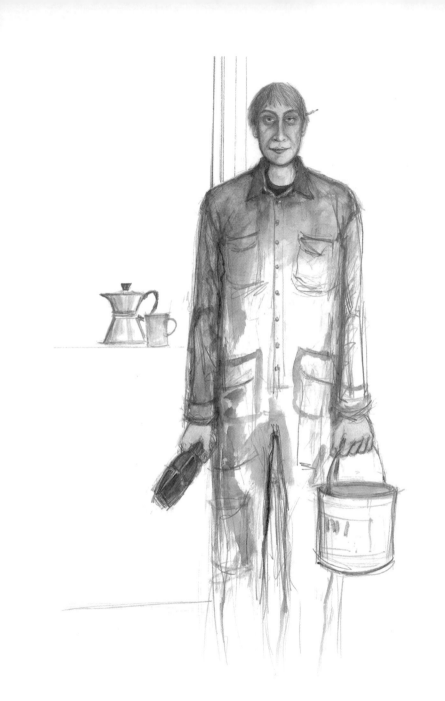

*He's the only person who politely puts his cardboard coffee cup
in the bin*

The Polish Handyman

KAROL IS A model of decorum. Fenella Fusspot, who was armed with her How to Deal with Builders guide, including strictures on loo-use (please flush) and smoking (please do not put ends down loo because they don't flush), was disarmed when Karol arrived with a novel, not the *Daily Mirror*. When Mark the Sparks (English) fuses all the electrics, quite his speciality, it is Karol who lopes off to Costa Coffee and brings cappuccinos back for everyone. He's the only person, other than Fenella, who then puts his cardboard cup in the bin. 'British builders just drop their rubbish where they stand,' Fenella says. She is now in handyman heaven.

Fenella is so pathetically grateful for Karol's consideration – he walks through the house in his socks so as not to dirty her new wooden floors – that she is now making him sandwiches for lunch. They sit in the rubble that will be the kitchen and Fenella, who is rarely interested in anything other than her nauseous children's exploits in extra maths, is humbled by Karol's polite English and halting explanations of his family background. 'You children could learn from Karol. His parents were doctors, he's been through university and he's come here to earn money so that he can study music.'

When Karol smokes, it is always outside; nor does he answer his mobile indiscriminately. Fenella is so used to her husband foraging in his pocket and shouting 'Yes?' to a Nokia that this politesse is overwhelming. Karol also says her Farrow & Ball paint is wonderful to work with, when her husband said it was too bloody expensive and Bernie the builder asked why 'just because it's called Sludge or Muck, or summat fashionable, it's better than Crown'? Karol understands. Fenella will write a reference for his music course, and be decidedly snappy with the school-run mothers on the subject of East European immigration.

The Bank Statement

IT CAN'T BE true. Quite obviously Coutts has got it all wrong. This is someone else's bank statement, nothing to do with Charlotte. Nothing. That really inferior suede skirt, which she now hates, could not possibly have cost £795 in MaxMara. She absolutely thought it was £195 – it is so not her fault if they print the prices so illegibly. Shouldn't the bank be able to do something about it? And what on earth was Aventura Limousine for £175.92? It appears to be when she was in Florida, but dollars and pounds are so confusing, and Charlotte thought anything in dollars was supposed to be so cheap. Surely it should be £17.59? Oh dear.

One might dispense with fresh flowers, but then everyone would notice that the drawing-room walls need painting. Truly, economy is so false. The absolute necessity is not to let her husband see the bank statement, because then he will come up with boring questions about The Wolseley – 'I thought it was supposed to be reasonable, but why have we an entry for £105? Treating that dreadful brother of yours again, Charlotte? Or is it a different Wolseley?' – thus she stuffs the telltale bank statements into the teapot. Which is absolutely fine until he makes tea. 'We seem to have Lapsang Overdraft here, dear.'

Charlotte is awfully sorry, she'll never do it again. Yes, hair colour with Gary at John Frieda really does cost £205. It is the only sum she recognises with indelible accuracy and happily acknowledges as money well spent. Upbraid her with suede skirts and limousines, but there is a point beyond which Charlotte cannot be pushed. It is her hair. 'There is no point in cheap hair colour. Gary should be sanctified. Everyone says my hair is marvellous. That my income is infinitely less than my tax is entirely Gordon Brown's fault.'

Charlotte thought anything in dollars
was supposed to be so cheap

Tracey is wondering whether she's got compulsive sudoku syndrome

The Sudoku Addicts

THE UNDERGROUND CARRIAGE is hushed. Mrs Penge is doing the *Daily Mail's* Code Number. Opposite her, Joseph is tackling the *Independent's* super-sized mind-scrambler with its 256 spaces. Tracey from accounts is chewing her pencil and ruminating over the *Guardian*; Mr Turbot's Daks suit is covered in eraser crumbs, as he's been wrestling with *The Times* since catching the 7.45 from Woking.

Sudoku is a welcome distraction on the Tube, although the gent with the earring had an alarming sudoku moment at Embankment when he realised he had two eights in the same row. Mrs Penge had the same trouble yesterday with her fives and overshot her stop at Gloucester Road; today she's resolved to save her sudoku for her coffee break. Tracey is wondering whether she's got compulsive sudoku syndrome, what Dean in the postroom told her about yesterday. Dean said his sister can't get her kids' breakfast any more, not till she's done her SunDoku in the *Sun*. Seems weird that some-thing invented by a blind Swiss geezer should have done for Dean's sister in Dollis Hill. The little boy who got on at Sloane Square is slicing and dicing according to Carol Vorderman's easy puzzle tips; he and his grandmother – a great *Countdown* fan – bought Carol's *How To Do Sudoku* in Waterstone's and have enthusiastically embraced her golden technique for intersecting the mini-grids.

At South Ken Joseph cracks it; his fellow passengers 'in the zone' recognise the look of beatific triumph, the secret smile, the rush of adrenalin as his magic squares form their perfect symmetry of logic and mathematics. Mr Singh, a loyal *Telegraph* puzzle-solver, shakes his turban sorrowfully – will he have the same success by South Ealing? Rubik's Cube was never like this.

Harry does not do good-for-you, or foreign,
or mushrooms, or green

The Fussy Eater

HARRY ADAMANTLY STICKS to white food. Only the tentative suggestion that he might remove his iPod at the dining-room table pierces his surly hormonal teenage indifference like an aberrant piece of broccoli. 'What's this, Mum?' 'It's good for you, Harry.' Harry does not do good-for-you, or foreign, or mushrooms, or green. Especially green. Harry is pasta, pizza and Pringles. And chips. Preferably pasta or pizza with chips. When his long-suffering mother cooks free-range roast chicken (white) and roast potatoes, he drowns the lot in ketchup. She has been known to weep in the kitchen. After breastfeeding, Magimixing Harry's baby food and sending him to kindergarten with lunchboxes of hummus and carrot sticks, she is harbouring a nutritional serpent, Jamie Oliver's worst nightmare. Her sister says all teenagers are like this. 'Which is not an excuse, I know, Louisa, but 80 per cent of households in some godforsaken part of northern England don't even have a table, they just graze at the fridge.'

Harry would be thrilled. How often does he mooch into the kitchen, hands stuffed in the pockets of his filthy combats, and say, 'Chelsea are playing Real Madrid tonight, Mum, I really need to eat in front of the telly'? Just when she's laid the table and lit candles. The result is an apocalyptic explosion by Harry's father on manners and how, if this is just a stage, Harry had damn well better get over it, 'and take that bloody thing out of your ears when I'm speaking to you'. Louisa finds it hard to imagine a future upstanding young man with whom it'll be possible to eat in public. How mystifying that the teenager who slouches in his chair, puts his elbows on the table, feigns ignorance of how to use a knife and fork, is umbilically linked to the ketchup bottle and eats with his mouth open for the full tumble-dryer effect, is inevitably at Eton.

The Female Hiker

ESME HAS TRODDEN the Trossachs and yomped many a Munro. Nothing more beautiful than the Highlands, despite her forays into Alp and Himalaya. Ben Boggle, Ben Elton, Ben Gargle: all have sustained the sturdy tread of her boots, rubber soles rutted as deep as a Nairobi car tyre. She has route-marched to Santiago de Compostela, not for Esme the pampering excess of pretend hiking, from the Michelin-starred restaurants to Relais & Chateaux hotels as purveyed to Gap-wearing Americans.

On her way to Compostela Esme stayed in pilgrims' hostels; the hard bed and the lumpy pillow are as nothing to one who has charged over 30 miles, sturdy of thigh and with a song in her heart, and can thus sleep the sleep of the just. The amateur hikers tread primrose paths on spring herbs under gnarled olive trees in Andalusia, a gentle amble culminating in a picnic and a snooze, but Esme has hiked from the Pyrenees to the Garrotxa through the ancient volcanoes of the Mediterranean hills.

Intriguing place, Catalonia, totally unspoilt. Esme doesn't do spoilt or noise. Give her the fells of Finland or the granite coast of Brittany. Many is the time she has arrived in a remote village in Nepal to be greeted by stunned natives who, once they have overcome their fear of her appearance, are deeply intrigued by her first-aid kit. Eminently capable, and always equipped with essential words of the local dialect, Esme has been on the RGS medical course and could, if pushed, take out her own appendix.

Done with the West Tyrol – far too Heidi – and appalled that swimming pools and spa complexes are now de rigueur in the meanest inns of the Bernese Oberland, Esme is heading for Tasmania. Splendidly wet and frightfully good wine. There are some things on which she certainly will not compromise.

She's charged over 30 miles, sturdy of thigh and with a song in her heart

The digging classes nurture Swiss chard, basil, sweetcorn,
and buddleia for the butterflies

The Allotment Holders

TOM FISHBURN, A retired university lecturer, is a new arrival. He had to wait seven years and was abandoning hope of an allotment in Camden, fearing he might have to brave Harrow, where the urge to grow Swiss chard, basil and artichokes untouched by chemicals is not so imperative as to have made allotments unobtainable. He's delighted to have joined the digging classes, has shared his sweetcorn crop and listens sympathetically to Deirdre's longings for her imminent retirement. 'Can't come soon enough. I'm a doctor, not a "medical operative", and I don't want to be part of the New Labour jumbo surgery.'

At times like these, Francesco is a dab hand with the coffee. His shed is known as The Caff. Having married an English girl, Francesco came to London from Naples in the 1970s. The coffee from Naples issa the besta in all of Italy. Francesco gives sound advice on tomatoes ('those in Naples are the besta'). Only lemons, another outstanding denizen of southern Italy, have sadly defeated him in Camden. Francesco has thus turned his attention to the borlotti bean. So healthy. Deirdre is nurturing buddleias for the butterflies, and Minty has her wildflowers and a brambly pond for the birds to drink. 'We are a utopian lifeline for urban sanity, not a glorified vegetable patch.' All are horrified that the Manor Gardens Allotments in Hackney Wick, an oasis of plum trees, wildlife and green-fingered new-age therapists, may be bulldozed to make way for the 2012 Olympic hockey pitches.

Meanwhile Tom is gathering his crop for their annual harvest-festival party. Francesco will augment Deirdre's rhubarb wine with some sound Italian red, they'll eat waxy potatoes and French beans, and hope the council isn't going to sell their utopia as a property development.

She owes it to Joshua's future to recycle bottles and old invitations

The Manic Recycler

EMILY'S EPIPHANY CAME courtesy of the *Ecologist*. One article on diminishing fish stocks and she was beset with fear that little Joshua might not live to eat a Dover sole. Then there's the depravity of importing mangetout from Tanzania and the outrageous anomaly of the all-year-round strawberry. Regardless of the fact that her SUV guzzles gas and all her televisions are on standby, thus consuming vast amounts of energy, Emily is now an avenging eco-angel. She owes it to Joshua, and has burrowed under the sink to retrieve the heinous orange bags in which Wandsworth Council wants her to recycle bottles and newspapers. When it says 'All clean paper and card', does that include old invitations?

Emily the eco-spy covertly inspects the neighbours' orange bags on recycling day. No. 17 only drinks Evian, whereas one can be woken at dawn by the clunk-clunk of No. 24 putting out the merry contents of Oddbins. At No. 3 (the last house in the street without plantation shutters and Ocado deliveries) they have far too many pizza boxes and Coke cans. Emily will never again threaten Joshua's future with fizzy drinks. From now on they are into Slow Cuisine, eating organic fruit and vegetables in season.

Bring back the paper bag is all Emily asks, as she takes the evil supermarket tyrant's plastic horrors back to the checkout to be recycled in aid of St Michael's Hospice. But then is paper politically correct in view of vanishing rainforests? Emily spends much of her time – and the daily's, at £10 an hour – removing staples from credit card statements so they can be recycled for the common good. It's so tiring she'll have to have one of her four annual holidays, using an aeroplane which consumes enough non-sustainable fuel on the way to India to feed all the beggars outside her Taj hotel.

The Animal Aunt

IT'S THE BUSIEST time of year for Auntie Pam. Buffer the boxer's Mummy and Daddy are on their yacht in Sardinia. Buffer has his pet passport, his claws aren't deck-friendly. 'You didn't fancy it much either, did you, pet?' says Auntie Pam comfortingly, and Buffer is now blissfully asleep on her sofa rather than skittering on varnished teak. Smith's and Wesson's Mummy is in her villa in Tuscany, where she hasn't dared take a dog since there was a viper invasion in the swimming pool. 'Smith and Wesson are such game little chaps, Auntie Pam. Like all Jack Russells they'd tackle anything. Then one might have to deal with a foreign vet.'

Auntie Pam is used to indulging the whims of demented dog owners. 'Now, Lady Throbbing, what does dear little Mitzi call outies?' 'Outies, of course.' 'Marvellous, so important to be on-message. Does Mitzi also do walkies and din-dins?' Mitzi, dozing now on Auntie Pam's comfy acetate-nylon shagpile slipper, is actually a yummies person. 'You say "yummies" and she's not to have anything except brown rice and free-range chicken. We do not do choc drops at night; Mitzi only likes Green & Black's organic chocolate. We do not spoil Mitzi, Auntie Pam, but of course she will sleep on your bed.'

Auntie Pam often wonders if she will run out of bed; there's Twizzle, her own sweetie-ratty grey whippet. Buffer is a pillow-hogger, Smith and Wesson are burrowers. Mitzi thinks the snowy folds of the duvet are too wonderful compared with Lady Throbbing's hairy tartan blankets. Auntie Pam gets their pills down them wrapped in pâté. In her Barbour jacket pocket there is always a little treat (Meaty Mice bikkies are popular) to encourage walkies. Her garden is full of the splendid smells of previous guests; she even has a cat for them to chase. The dogs' parents are on holiday; so are they.

Auntie Pam is used to indulging the whims
of demented dog owners

*The vicar sees Audrey Sloley, who's supposed to be helping him
with evensong, taking too keen an interest in the sloe gin*

The Village Fete

ADELE SOWERBY HAS been winkling bottles out of the parish for weeks. 'Come on now, Colonel, we all know you have a special friendship with Messrs Gordon – why don't you slip me a splendid green bottle? By the time I've importuned Mrs Moffat's bridge four and Lady Herriard's butler we could have 12 green bottles a-hanging on the wall.' People have dived into the darkest recesses of their cellars and produced ageing framboise, which tasted so marvellous in the south of France, and long-lost Metaxa, a virulent Greek brandy which anaesthetised the fried octopus so well. Not that there is much octopus in Bagpuize Magna. The Partridges thankfully parted with the wine in a funny-shaped bottle that the Birds brought to them for supper, having been given it by the Plovers when they came to supper with them.

The vicar, on his way to bless the Comical Dog Show, is alarmed to see that Audrey Sloley, who's supposedly helping him with even-song at Upton Bagpuize, is taking a keen interest in the sloe gin. Mrs Threadgold has had a sell-out on the cake stall, because although everyone worships Nigella – imagine if she were to open the fete, someone at the PCC did say their best friend knew a friend of hers – no one can make a Victoria sponge any more. Mrs Threadgold thus feels vastly superior to bric-a-brac (chipped china ornaments), the plant stall (wilting clematis) and books, where everyone has dumped their old paperbacks.

Health and safety regulations have made the egg-and-spoon race virtually impossible, and animal cruelty conspired against bowling for the pig. Tilly Sloley is crying because Archie Sowerby butted her on the bouncy castle. The vicar, limping because he's been bitten by Lady Herriard's Pekingese, considers whether 'Fetes worse than death' would be an amusing subject for his next sermon.

The Maid of Honour

NICOLA IS AWARE that mauve is not her colour. She also knows that the marvellous little woman in Compton Foliat ('She used to work for Belinda Bellville, you know') has made a dress of surreal hideousness, in which Nicola's bottom is going to appear as a gigantic satin prune wobbling up the aisle. Never has bringing up the rear been more poignant. There's the niggling suspicion that she was chosen to be maid of honour because she wasn't prettier than the bride. Whom she adores, of course. They were at St Mary's together, homesick on the first night, clutching their teddies. Then Newcastle University, sick on Pinot Grigio and clutching Teddy in various sweaty bars. There he is now, suave in his morning suit at the top of the aisle, gazing at his bride as she floats towards him on clouds of bliss. This could have been Nicola's day. She and Teddy had their little moment – not that the bride knows.

Why, oh why is everyone married except Nicola? July is an agonising month for her; each weekend is a wedding. She's bought a zillion presents at the White Company. Even the best man and all the ushers are married, so her traditional role in today's celebration, that of being snogged out by the Portaloos, seems unlikely to be fulfilled. Why won't Simon marry her? They've lived together for two years, her parents keep asking What's Going On?, and Nicola has mentally planned the wedding right down to lavender strewn on the floor of the marquee, the scent to be freshly crushed by a hundred LK Bennett kitten heels. The placemats will be photocopied pictures of Simon and herself as children. She'll lose weight. Great Aunt Maud's tiara will be allowed out of the bank. Her bridesmaids will all be *little ones* in frothing white organdie. How she has dreamed, but she can't even catch the bride's bouquet because she's hobbled by the hideous dress.

There's the niggling suspicion that she was chosen to be maid
of honour because she wasn't prettier than the bride

Olive knows she dresses like Maria
from The Sound of Music

The Downtrodden Wife

OLIVE IS AGED 47 and has never had her own bank account. Reggie Pettigrew doesn't believe in that sort of nonsense. Mr Pettigrew, who is senior assistant (metric) of Woldshire County Council's Weights and Measures department, likes to know where every one of his hard-earned pennies – or rather pence – has gone. Not for Olive the secret splurge on a new dress from A La Mode. On the last Sunday of the month, after a proper lunch with meat and two veg, he likes nothing better than to sit down with Olive's household accounts. As a result she haunts the supermarket's Buy One Get One Free chill cabinets. While Mr Pettigrew is policing Woldshire's farmers' markets for signs of aberrant sales in pounds and ounces, Olive is scouring Somerfield for a discounted chicken on the cusp of its sell-by date.

Her battered satchel handbag – containing a separate purse for Housekeeping Money – was given to her by her daughter for her 40th birthday. In her heart she knows she dresses like Maria from *The Sound of Music*, but the social demands of weights and measuring require little else than a rayon jungle print from Marks & Spencer, *circa* 1989. It does very well for the occasional cocktail function at the golf club with the scions of middle management: bank managers, accountants, insurance brokers in grey shoes. Their second wives are in remarkably *Footballers' Wives* attire, but Reggie would certainly not like Olive to attempt high heels or an exciting mid-knee hemline. She tentatively suggested that she might take a job reading to the children in the local kindergarten (inspired by a vision of Her Own Money), but Mr Pettigrew asked what would happen if he wished to come home for lunch. Once Olive was a lively spark in AmDram, but her get up and go long since got up and left.

The Ghillie

MURDO MCTAVISH HAS the patience of all the saints. Murdo's stoic presence has reassured many a callow Sassenach that he could catch a salmon the size of a whale. The dark pools and whirling eddies of the Findhorn are his lore. Master Geordie (now aged 45) cannot remember a time when Murdo was not there to show him, yet again, how to tie a spiggled bunny thrush fly. There was the day when, as a child, he had caught no fish and Murdo said gently, 'Next time, Master Geordie, you bring a wee box with you.' And so he did, and Murdo told him it was his box of patience. 'And if the fish take their time, you open it a wee bit, and a wee bit of patience will come out.'

He is a rock of ages in estate tweed in which he will crawl through the heather up Glen Campbell in search of a fine stag. The ardent sportsman puffing behind knows better than to question Murdo as he is told to crouch in a peaty quagmire with a burn running down the back of his neck. 'You can only get as wet as your skin, sir.' The production of a BlackBerry during the picnic seems absurd in the presence of this modest god of nature. 'Er, it's marvellous, Murdo, you can get your e-mails.' 'Och aye, sir,' he says impassively, and retires a little way away to eat his piece, a floury white bap with thick slices of ham, made by Mrs McTavish.

Never ever, on the hill or by the river, will he drink; that is for later, in front of the fire with the *Press & Journal*. The dreadful state of the grouse this year, the dangerous absurdity of the Right to Roam, these are subjects that distress Murdo. Only the other day he had a marvellous beast in his sights for the laird, when a mithering rambler came across the moor in a pink cagoule. The river is his solace; the silvery, eternal waters. Master Geordie still has his wee box of patience.

He is a rock of ages in estate tweed

The Jigsaw Puzzlers

TARA AND JAMIE are well pissed off. They were doing brilliantly on the jigsaw, having sorted out the edge, until Aunt Cassandra and Uncle Iain wobbled along after lunch and took over.

Mummy always sets up a jigsaw in the hall at Christmas, on a bridge table, but she doesn't mean it to distract everyone from Clearing Up. 'We always give the staff Christmas Day off,' she says loudly, clashing dirty plates of turkey together, regardless of the fact that she doesn't have staff. 'Do put a bit of sky in for me,' is her final shot as she reverses through the kitchen door, bottom first, her arms laden with dead crackers and wilted party hats.

Aunt Cassie and Uncle Iain – backs to domestic chaos – are saying how wonderful it is to have a real family Christmas, and what fun it will be watching the Queen's speech. 'Now, Jamie, never underestimate what it is to be British. You may think the Queen is an old fossil, but let me tell you she is a National Treasure.' Jamie recognises an over-refreshed adult when he sees one, has always thought the Queen to be the only consistent grown-up in the world, and doesn't wish to be patronised by someone who's dithering about with a yellowy-firey bit of Turner's *Fighting Temeraire*.

Tara can't believe Uncle Iain's shirt. Saddo. Aunt Cassie rather overdid the Dom Perignon before lunch and keeps laughing hysterically as she tries to force bits of jigsaw puzzle together, creating that hump effect of the amateur, bashing it flat with her rings. 'It really does fit, I promise, it has to, I think it's a bit of the mast of the *Temerararah*. Hic.'

Then Iain knocks his glass of red wine over the puzzle, and all the sticky-out bits curl at the edges and go crisp while being dried on the Aga.